Little Mitchie

SNAILS THAT CARRY THEIR HOUSES

TINY BUT MIGHTY!

TRACY VONDER BRINK

CREATING YOUNG NONFICTION READERS

Little Mitchie books spark curiosity and support early nonfiction reading for students in Grades 2-3. Designed to build vocabulary, support second language learners, and prepare readers for middle-grade content, each book includes helpful tips for parents and educators to build confidence and deepen understanding of the world.

TIPS FOR READING NONFICTION WITH BEGINNING READERS

Talk about Nonfiction

Begin by explaining that nonfiction books give us information that is true. The book will be organized around a specific topic or idea, and we may learn new facts through reading.

Look at the Parts

Most nonfiction books have helpful features. Our *Little Mitchie* titles include color photographs and graphic aids, a table of contents, a glossary, and an index. Share the purpose of these features with your reader.

Color Photos and Graphic Aids

A lot of information can be found by "reading" photos, charts, maps, and other graphic aids found within nonfiction texts. Help your reader learn more about the different ways information can be displayed.

Table of Contents

Located at the front of the book, this list shows the big ideas within the text and the page numbers where they can be found.

Glossary

Located at the back of the book, the glossary defines key words and phrases that are related to the topic. These words and phrases can be found in the text in colored type.

Index

Located at the back of the book, an index is an alphabetical list of topics and the page numbers where they can be found.

With a little help and guidance about reading nonfiction, you can feel good about introducing a young reader to the world of *Little Mitchie* nonfiction books.

Little Mitchie is an imprint of:

Mitchell Lane
PUBLISHERS

2001 SW 31st Avenue
Hallandale, FL 33009
mitchelllanepub.com

First Edition, 2027.

Author: Tracy Vonder Brink
Designer: Jen Bowers
Editor: Tricia Hoffman

Library of Congress Cataloging-in-Publication Data
Title: Snails That Carry Their Houses /
by Tracy Vonder Brink

Description: Hallandale, FL :
Mitchell Lane Publishers, [2027]

Identifiers:
ISBN 979-8-89260-887-9 (library bound)
ISBN 979-8-89260-990-6 (eBook)

Library of Congress Control Number: 2026936529

PHOTO CREDITS
Shutterstock: cover, p.1 ©2018 Andrei Armiagov, p.5 ©2021 sasha pepper, p.6 ©2025 Bob Hilscher, p.9 ©2010 ivosar, p.10–11 ©2021 Molnar Sebestyen, p.12 ©2010 lukko, p.15, 22 ©2023 BirdShutterB, p.16 ©2009 Serg64, p.17, 22 ©2009 AnutkaT, p.18, 22 ©2008 goran cakmazovic, p.21 ©2006 Stephen Rees

TABLE OF CONTENTS

Chapter One

HOME SWEET SHELL

The shadow of a flying bird falls over a snail. Birds eat snails! The snail pulls itself inside its shell to keep its body safe.

MIGHTY MOMENT

Snails come in different shapes, colors, and sizes. The smallest is tinier than a grain of sand. The biggest is almost three feet (91 cm) long.

Snails live on land and in the water. They belong to a group of animals called **mollusks**. All mollusks make their own shells. How do snails do it?

Chapter Two

LET'S LOOK AT A SNAIL

A snail never leaves its shell. The shell is part of its body. All of a snail's **organs** are inside its shell. The hard shell protects the soft organs.

A layer of soft **tissue** called the mantle covers the **inner** shell wall. The mantle helps protect the organs. It also makes the shell.

MIGHTY MOMENT

Some kinds of snail shells have a lid. The snail can pull in its body and close the lid behind it.

The snail's body has a head and a foot. The head pokes out of the front of the shell. The foot is underneath the snail's body.

Chapter Three

SHELL SECRETS

A snail hatches with a tiny shell that's almost see-through. The snail needs **calcium** to make the shell grow. Land snails eat plants or soil that have it. Sea snails take in calcium from ocean water.

MIGHTY MOMENT

Newly-hatched snails eat their own eggshells for their first calcium. They may also eat eggs that haven't hatched yet.

The mantle adds new layers of shell each time the snail grows. The mantle puts down layers of new shell around where the snail's head pokes out. The newest part of a shell is always at the opening.

mantle

MIGHTY MOMENT
Most snails' shells curve to the right. A few go to the left.

The layers **curve** up as the mantle adds them. A layer is called a whorl when it wraps all the way around in a circle. How many whorls a shell has depends on the kind of snail. For example, a brown-lipped snail has four or five whorls.

Chapter Four

SUPER SNAILS

Snails pull their bodies inside their shells to stay safe. They also sleep there. A snail is never far from home!

MIGHTY MOMENT

Many snails can go all the way inside their shells, but not all. Some kinds of snails' bodies are too big to fit!

A CLOSER LOOK

Snail eggs look like bubbles of clear jelly. Most kinds hatch in about two to four weeks.

The color of a snail's shell can match where it lives. This helps it hide from predators.

The mantle not only makes the snail's shell—it also helps the snail breathe!

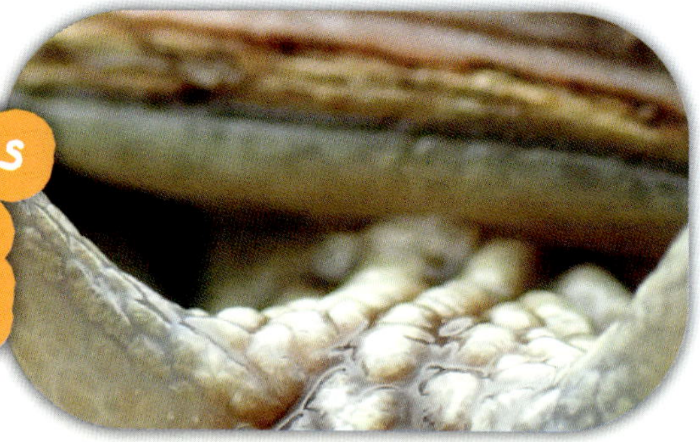

GLOSSARY

calcium (kal-see-uhm) a mineral that builds strong body parts such as bones and teeth

curve (kurv) a smooth bend in one direction without any sharp corners

inner (in-ur) inside

mollusks (mah-luhsks) kinds of animals that have soft bodies, no backbones, and usually a shell

organs (or-guhnz) parts of the body made of different tissues that work together

tissue (tish-oo) a group of similar cells that form a certain part or organ

FURTHER READING

Emminizer, Theresa. *Slimy Snails*. Enslow Publishing, 2024.

Podmorow, Ava. *Snails*. Engage Books, 2023.

ON THE INTERNET

Snails
www.in.gov/dnr/kids/animals/fish/snails/
Indiana's Department of Natural Resources tells you about snails' bodies and how they move.

Snail and Slug
https://kids.britannica.com/kids/article/snail-and-slug/353784
Learn about the differences between snails and slugs with Britannica Kids.

INDEX